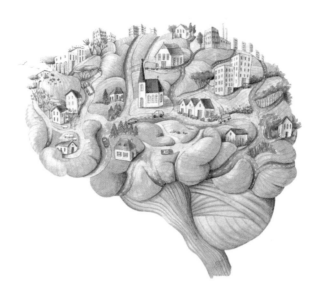

✎ NAME:

Published by Olimpia Mesa / Instructional Design Ltd
http://howpeoplelearnbook.com

Illustrated by Irina Neacsu
Book and cover design by Denisa Nastase

Before you learn anything, it can be helpful to learn about yourself.

⭐ Vlad Mesa, age 11

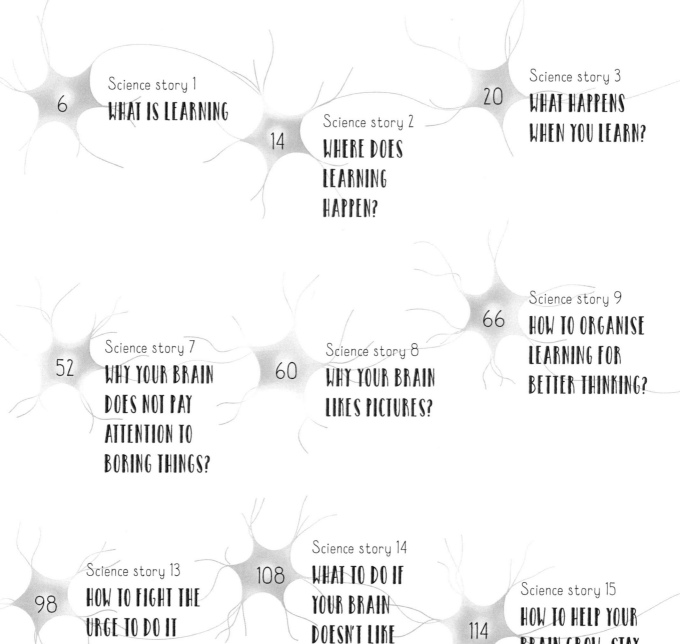

WHAT IS LEARNING

The book you hold in your hands is about learning. So, let's find out what you think learning is. Take a look at the pictures and select which ones you believe are learning activities.

When I first asked my son to do this, he said, 'I am only going to mark this one where children learn in school.' Many other children did the same thing, but scientists say learning includes all the other actions too.

We all learned highly complex skills before we ever entered a classroom. We learned to understand and speak a language. We learned to roll over, crawl, stand up, balance and walk. We also learned to amuse, annoy, befriend, argue and ask questions.

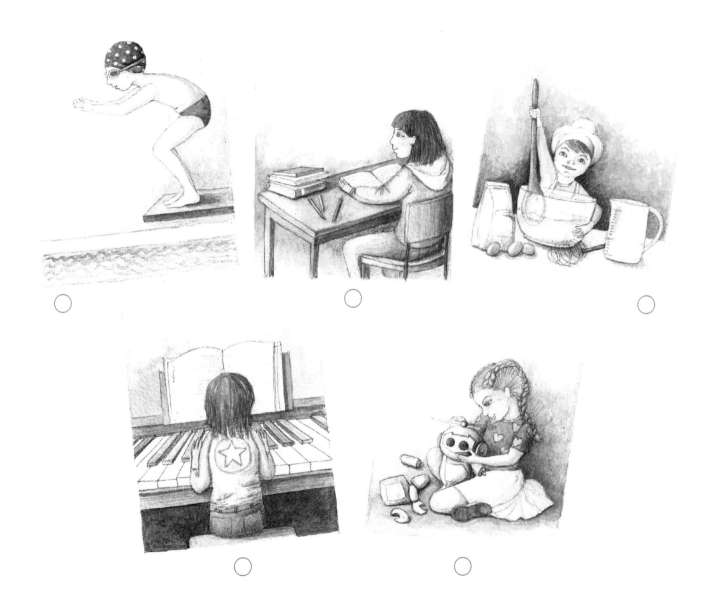

Did you ask questions before you started school? I bet you did. We all, children and adults alike, have a natural desire to learn. Just because you happened to turn six one day, doesn't mean that is the moment when you started to learn. Scientists say learning is a natural process. It starts when we are born and lasts a lifetime.

There are many different ways of learning. It's not only in school that you learn. We learn a great deal on our own when we observe the world around us. We learn when we play. We learn when we interact with other people. We also learn when we do things, experimenting and adapting as we go.

When I was a child, my mother taught me how to use a sewing machine. By the age of ten, I had more than 100 outfits for my ballerina doll. I learned by observing and paying attention to what my mother was doing. I also developed my skills through trial and error. To create so many outfits, I had to learn to sketch them on paper, measure accurately and cut the material. To be able to do this, I had to understand units of measurement, as well as know about different types of yarns. Eventually, I added knitting and crochet too. Like riding a bike, once learned, these skills have stayed with me and I still use them today. Instead of buying new clothes, I repair and adjust many of them myself.

There are many different ways to learn. If you continue reading, you will discover several of them. You do not have to learn in the same way that your friends do. You can choose your own strategies and experiment. Learning how to learn is your superpower.

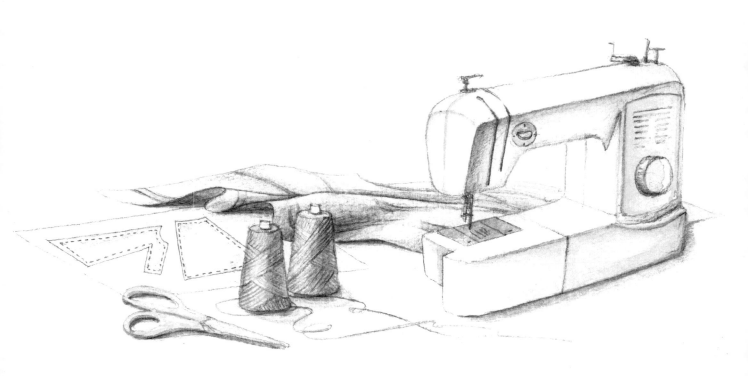

TRY THIS:

Write a list of everything you've learned so far in your life. Try to remember who or what helped you learn them.

Write another list of what you really want to learn in the future. Think of a person or resource that can help you.

DOODLE HERE:

WHERE DOES LEARNING HAPPEN?

Look at your own body, then at the picture on the next page. Mark where you think learning happens. When I was a little girl and started going to dance classes, I thought that learning happened in my legs. Later on, I discovered in science books that there was so much more to it than that. Learning to dance is about more than the legs, just as learning to play the piano is about more than the hands and learning to speak another language is about more than the mouth.

Scientists say that all learning takes place in *the brain*. Everything we know now and will learn in the future happens mostly in this magnificent organ situated in our heads.

The outside of your brain is covered with wrinkly folds called *gyri*. On the inside, your brain has a lot of parts that help you walk, talk, see, hear, breathe and think. By using your brain, you control everything you do, everything you think or feel.

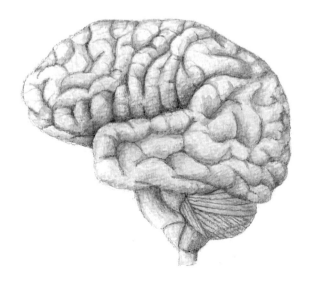

You might think that a computer is the best thing in the world, that it's super speedy and can do everything. Well, it can't. Imagine a situation in the park when you see your friend stumbling on something and ready to fall. What happens is first your eyes see the friend approaching the dangerous object. The information your eyes provide helps the brain understand how quickly you need to react. Then your muscles jump into action and help you to save your friend from falling. The brain enables such a rapid response in a way that no computer ever could. The brain is much more powerful.

The brain weighs about 3 pounds (1.3 kg) and is a wrinkly, pink organ that some scientists say feels like soft mushroom. It is about 6 inches long (15 cm), about 5.5 inches wide (14 cm) and nearly 4 inches deep (10 cm).

TRY THIS:

Watch the video tutorial at
http://www.howpeoplelearnbook.com/tutorials about how
to draw a brain. Create your own poster about the brain,
using the title 'My Brain – an amazing organ!'

DOODLE HERE:

WHAT HAPPENS WHEN YOU LEARN?

Everything we know now and will learn in the future is a result of capturing the information around us. Information is brought to the brain through elaborate systems. Let's imagine that our brain consists of millions of imaginary roads, with millions of imaginary cars travelling on them very quickly, all the time. These machines carry information to different areas of the brain.

There are many of these areas, each storing different types of information. You know a phone is ringing, for example, or a dog barking in the street, because the information has been sent to the special area of the brain where similar information is held for whenever you need it. I think of these areas of the brain as houses. There are houses for information about words, numbers, feelings and so much more.

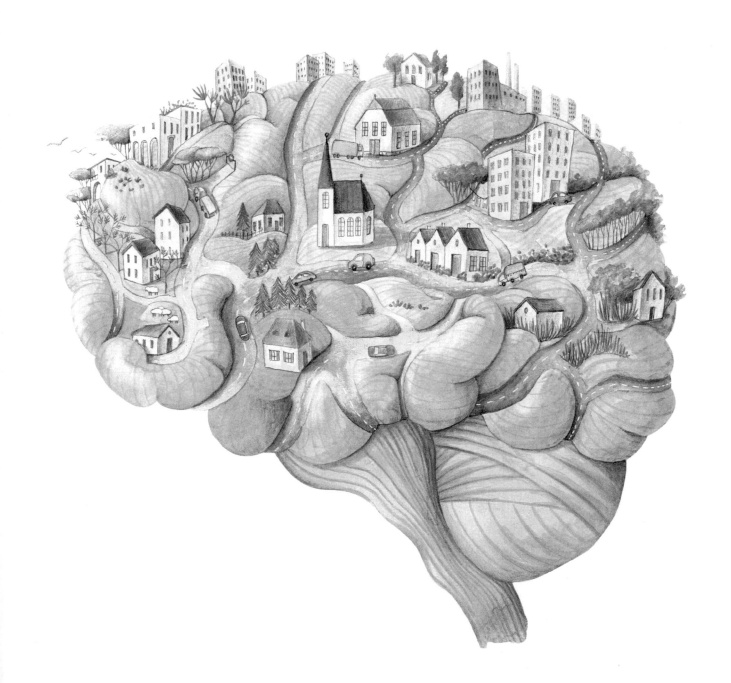

When you learn new things, it's like transporting information in cars on roads, heading for specific houses. Similarly, when you want to retrieve information that you learned a while ago, it's like sending a car to that particular house, collecting the information and driving it on fast roads to take it to where you need it.

These cars travel very quickly because there are no obstacles such as traffic lights or stop signs that stand in their way. Such a car can take less than a second to pick up the information from a house and deliver it to where you need it. The information is transported faster than the blink of an eye.

Sometimes when you find it's difficult to learn, it's as if some of the roads in the brain do not lead to the new house or are blocked by traffic jams. When you do not know the right address, or when cars are caught in heavy traffic, no one knows how long it will take for the information to reach its destination. But it will arrive if the cars persist in finding the right way, hopefully avoiding traffic.

When you have to write an essay at school, it can take a long time to put a few phrases down on a blank page. This is especially true when you write about something new to you. The road is not yet well known. In some cases, the cars may be slowed by the unmapped terrain on their journey to the knowledge house where words are kept.

Brain scientists call these roads in the brain *neural connections* and the houses are called *neurones*. The human brain contains more than one hundred billion neurones. Each neurone is connected to about one thousand of its neighbours. These trillions of connections form the entire network of roads in our brains. Every time you learn something new, the brain creates new neural connections. In other words, the brain develops continuously, creating new roads and new routes for the cars to follow.

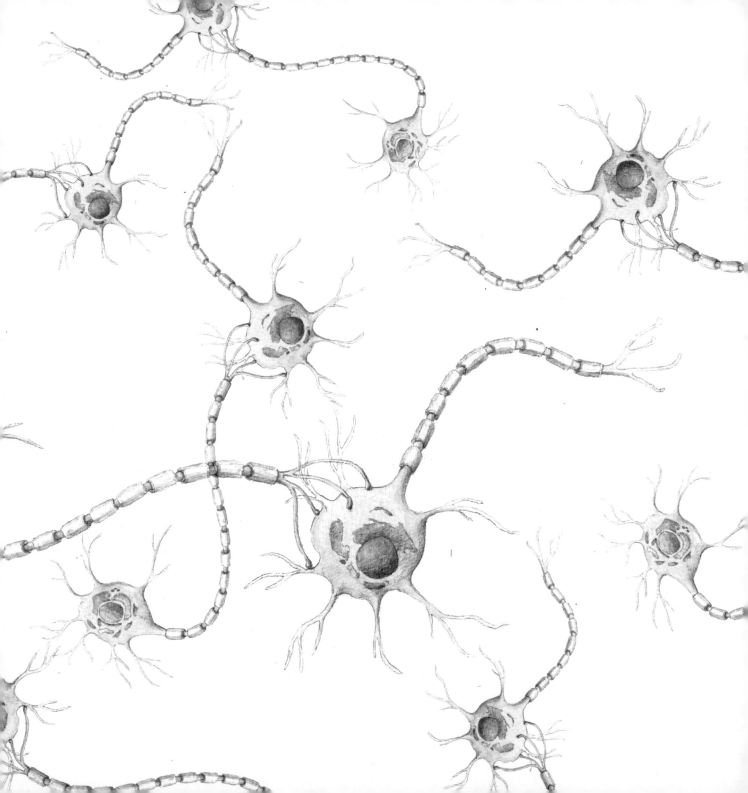

TRY THIS:

When you find it difficult to learn something new, don't give up. Take a small break, then try again. Give the cars time to discover new routes or for the roads to become unblocked.

Watch the video tutorial at http://www.howpeoplelearnbook.com/tutorials about how to create neurones from beads, rope or string.

DOODLE HERE:

THE BRAIN HAS MANY PARTS THAT DO ALL KINDS OF DIFFERENT JOBS!

Scientists say that a person has about 70,000 thoughts each day. This is a lot of work and it is managed by a part of your brain called the **cerebrum**.

Have a look at the picture of the brain. As you can see, the cerebrum is the biggest part of the brain. It controls your muscles and holds your memories.

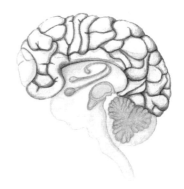

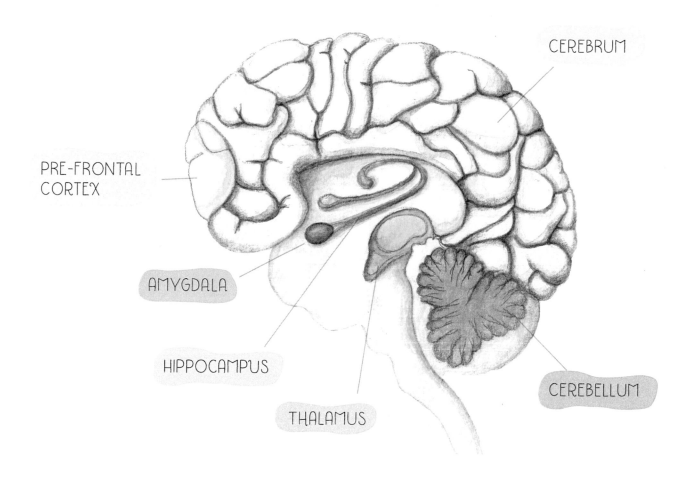

CEREBRUM

PRE-FRONTAL
CORTEX

AMYGDALA

HIPPOCAMPUS

THALAMUS

CEREBELLUM

Before we can think or learn, information about the outside world needs to find its way in through our senses to the brain. The **thalamus** is the gateway to the brain for all the information coming in when we see, hear, taste and touch.

The one sense that does not enter the brain through the thalamus is smell. It goes directly from your nose to your brain through a nerve.

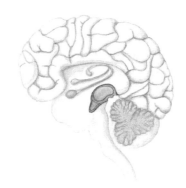

Next comes a part of the brain without which you would fall over: the **cerebellum**. It is a small but important area at the back of the brain that controls your balance and helps your muscles coordinate movement.

Think of a surfer riding the waves on his board. What does he need most to stay balanced? The best surfboard? The coolest wetsuit? No, he needs his cerebellum!

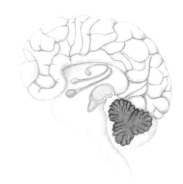

decide

Remember how people touch their forehead when they forget to do stuff? Do you do that too?

Did you know that the area of the brain behind your forehead, known as the **prefrontal cortex**, helps you make decisions, analyse and solve problems?

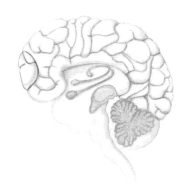

If you can't retain what you learned in your first year at school, the second is going to be pretty tricky, right? But don't worry. The **hippocampus**, which is the part at the centre of your brain, is like the GPS your parents use to find an address.

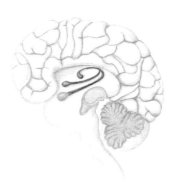

The hippocampus is in charge of remembering details and storing memories.

Do you ever wonder what happens when you get angry? Or why it is hard to calm down? Or why you do strange things that you might regret later? There is a small area of the brain in charge of this that is about the size of a walnut.

It is called the **amygdala** and allows you to feel big emotions. The amygdala also lets you know when you are in danger. It is very important for understanding other people's emotions too.

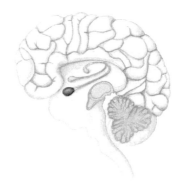

Scientists say that if you want to know how big your brain is, you can see by putting your two fists together. You need both fists because the brain has two halves. The left side of the brain controls the right half of the body, while the right side controls the left. Each half also controls specialised functions, dependent on whether you are left-handed or right- handed.

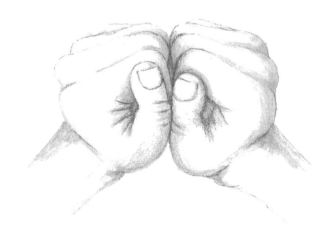

TRY THIS:

Put your fists side by side to see how big your brain is. Then draw a basic brain model. You can use different colours for the various parts and regions.

Show it to your friends and family, explaining how it works. A video tutorial is available at: http://www.howpeoplelearnbook.com/tutorials

DOODLE HERE:

LEARNING IS CHANGING THE BRAIN!

Think back to when you learned to ride a bike. It may have seemed like a hopelessly complicated process. You might have thought, 'I just don't have it in me. Biking isn't my thing.' But instead, you practised, practised, and practised some more. Now, biking is probably second nature, something you can do while singing. When I was ten years old, I had to learn French. It was so difficult at first that sometimes I questioned my own intelligence. Today, though, I speak four different languages fluently.

Scientists have shown that no one is born intelligent. So, how do people become more intelligent? They say the brain is like a physical muscle: it gets stronger the more you use it. In other words, to become smart requires as much practice as possible through reading, exercises, games and calculations. While lifting weights provides the muscles in your body with a workout, your brain is best exercised by trying to learn many different things.

When people stop practising new things, the brain will eventually eliminate the connections that formed the relevant pathways. As with a system of roads connecting various houses, the more cars going to a certain destination, the wider the road that carries them needs to be. The fewer cars travelling that way, however, the fewer lanes are required. Consequently, the unused parts of the brain are like vehicles abandoned in a car park, covered in dust and rust.

The good news is that when you use your brain to complete a task, the brain remembers the task, so the next time it becomes a little easier. The time after that, it's easier still, and so on.

It's also important to know that the brain does not grow just from getting the answers right. Mistakes can make the brain grow too. To keep strengthening neural pathways, we must continue challenging ourselves and going to the next level of difficulty. Scientists refer to the brain's ability to form new neural connections as *neuroplasticity* or *brain plasticity*. This refers to the brain's ability to change with learning. It does not mean that the brain is made of plastic!

Brain scientists are very knowledgeable about how we think, remember and learn.

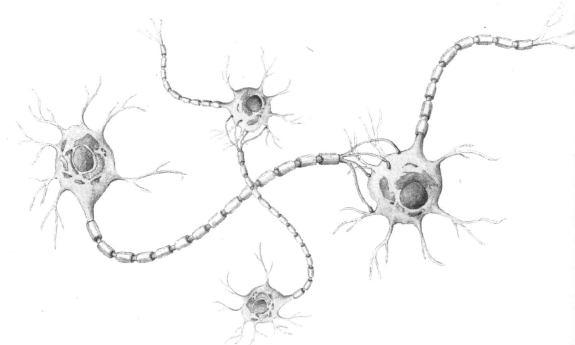

TRY THIS:

Make a list of activities that were once difficult for you but have become much easier with practice. Keep the list somewhere visible. When a task feels too hard, look at this list to remind yourself of all the things that were once difficult and are now second nature.

Watch the video tutorial at http://www.howpeoplelearnbook.com/tutorials about how to create a Brain Plasticity poster.
You can also create a poster to remind yourself to think like a scientist, including questions and statements like:

INSTEAD OF	I CAN SAY
I'm dumb	What am I missing?
This is too hard!	This will take a lot of effort!
They are smarter than me.	I want to learn their strategies!
I'm good at this.	How can I keep on improving?

WHY DOES YOUR BRAIN LIKE EXPLORING AND BREAKING STUFF?

I remember when I was five years old, I cut open a pillow to see what was inside it. Can you imagine how my room looked covered in feathers? Fortunately, my parents were not upset about it. From the age of four, my son began collecting our old household devices in order to take them apart and explore their inner workings. Have you ever broken anything because you were very curious? Have you tried to dismantle a broken clock, radio, laptop or tablet just to see what it looks like on the inside?

Scientists say this is normal behaviour as humans are natural-born explorers. There are many reasons why we explore. From birth, we learn about life and how it works by exploring. No brain can be satisfied for very long without exploring. Whether you are talking to someone, looking around the room or breaking stuff to see what's inside, you are exploring.

~ Rosaceae ~

1.   2.   3.

fig. A
Rosa Canina

Our brains are built to be curious about everything. We learn something new every day. That is the way we are. We like to understand things and how they work. Curiosity makes us explorers. This is a great thing because exploration looks forwards, not backwards. We don't want to be stuck in the past, we want to move ahead. Exploration gives us the sense that anything is possible. It leads to knowledge and understanding. That means you are constantly learning and making the world a better place.

TRY THIS:

If there were no schools but only self-learning, what would you study right now?

Create a list of things that you are curious about. Let other people know what you want to learn about. Share with them the questions you have about your world.

You can use the following sentence stems to make notes:

I wonder why _____ .

I wonder who _____ .

I've always been curious about _____

because _____ .

DOODLE HERE:

WHY YOUR BRAIN DOES NOT PAY ATTENTION TO BORING THINGS?

'I'm bored!' Have you ever counted how many times you say this phrase? My son estimates that he has this thought about ten times a week. Boredom is a universal experience. Almost everyone suffers from it. Some children define boredom as having nothing to do, some as a lack of interest in or difficulty concentrating on whatever it is they are supposed to be doing.

Brain scientists say that boredom can be caused by repetition and disinterest in the details of a task. For example, waiting in line at a cinema, a shop or an airport can be boring. In general, too much of the same thing can cause an absence of desire and a feeling of boredom.

Some children are more likely to be bored than others. Children and adults with a strong need for novelty, excitement and variety experience boredom more often than others. Scientists say that some people may take risks as a way to cure their boredom. The problem is that risk-taking can be dangerous.

TRY THIS:

Let other people know when you are bored but never expect them to fix the problem for you. Only your brain knows the solution to your boredom. Why not make a list of everything you enjoy doing or would like to try in the future? This could be written on a big poster in your room. You'll be able to look at it every time the thought 'I'm bored!' kicks in.

When we are bored, we can't pay attention. If this happens when you do your homework, try having a break every 25 minutes. You will find that going for a walk will help a lot too. If you are bored at school, you could focus on two or three questions you would like to ask your teacher. It is very important to speak up in class if you don't understand some-thing. Ask questions to get a better understanding of concepts and meanings.

Brains are not divided up into disciplines like school subjects. They prefer exploring real and natural phenomena that are not easily separated into categories. Try to imagine applying what your teacher talks about in the classroom to a real-life situation. If your teacher has discussed triangles, for example, ask yourself how triangles are used and why they are so important.

When you are in a queue for a long period of time and begin to feel bored, try these simple strategies. Imagine you are a scientist and check the labels on products to study what they are made from. Or imagine you are an architect or a designer. How would you improve the space you are in? What colours, fabrics or furniture would you use?

Create a personal journal. In this journal you could record all kinds of interesting things by mixing writing, drawing and collage. Here are some questions to start with:

What are the types of books, movies and games that you enjoy? What makes them so great?
What kind of games do not exist but should?
What issues do you care about and why?
What is one thing you wish you could change about the world?
What kind of toy or object do you wish you could make?

DOODLE HERE:

WHY YOUR BRAIN LIKES PICTURES?

How about an experiment? Invite friends and family to participate. Put ten pictures on a table, then cover them with a towel or cloth. Tell the participants that you have a number of pictures on the table and that you want them to remember as many items as possible. Also tell them that they will have only one minute to view them. Then take off the cover and use a clock, watch or phone to keep track of the time. After one minute, cover up the pictures. Ask the participants to name all the items that they can remember.

Repeat the same experiment, only this time, instead of using images, write ten words on a piece of paper. Ask the participants whether they found it easier to recall images or words. Which was more fun to play with?

Brain scientists say that our brains are naturally drawn to colour, contrast and movement. Because of this, pictures attract our attention more quickly and easily than words. Our brains learn and remember best through images, not through writing or speech. The reason pictures are so attractive may be very simple: our survival in the world depends very much on what we see around us.

Another surprising thing is that we treat text as images. As you read this paragraph, your brain is interpreting each letter as an image. This makes reading incredibly inefficient when compared to how quickly and easily we can take in information from a picture.

TRY THIS:

When you find what you are reading is difficult to understand and remember, use pencils and paper to draw or doodle what you see when you read each paragraph. What's the doodle that comes to mind when you are reading this science story?

Transform school reading material into flash cards with images on them. Add doodles, photos or pictures from magazines and newspapers to your notes. Use colours and diagrams to illustrate the new ideas you learn.

Some textbooks have too many pictures. This is no good for your brain. Use a blank piece of paper or card to cover parts of the page and reveal only the sections you want to focus on.

DOODLE HERE:

HOW TO ORGANISE LEARNING FOR BETTER THINKING?

I talk often with children like you about learning and thinking. Many are at their most enthusiastic when teachers use experiments to help them learn new information. For example, many of the children remembered how much they enjoyed a lesson on evaporation because the teacher invited them to experiment with water. Children were able to play the role of a scientist in a laboratory and create videos that showed particles changing from liquid to gas.

Brain scientists tell us that children's brains learn most readily and easily in a laboratory-like environment where they can experiment and discover things for themselves. All children are born creative, curious about the world and keen to try things out, exploring and playing.

Experiments that involve both action and observation help us process information in multiple parts of the brain at the same time. This also happens because when we experiment, we use many of our senses at once.

Better understanding and thinking also happens when our brains can see the big picture, providing context for what we learn. *Timelines* can be useful for this. They are graphic representations of the chronology of events over time. Let's say you learn about a famous queen. You know she lived a long time ago, but it will be difficult to remember when exactly if you do not have a timeline to refer to, helping you understand when she lived in relation to you and to other historical figures and events.

My Timeline

2009
My first cake

2010

2011
My first Holiday

2012
TEDDY

We know from research that your brain likes to connect thoughts. It connects every idea, memory or piece of information to tens, hundreds and even thousands of other ideas and concepts. This is how adult brains manage complicated projects at work or home. A good way to understand this is to consider the organisation of a birthday party, as illustrated by the mind map on the previous page.

A *mind map* is a visual overview of information which uses colours, words and images and connects related information to each other using branches. A mind map uses a similar structure to that found in the branches of trees or the neural pathways in our brains.

How well those ideas connect depends on you. To help your brain structure the new ideas and the information learned you could start by using mind maps yourself. For example, you can use a mind map to help you understand what you are reading for school. This involves taking the ideas that have formed in your head, then organising them into something visible and tree-like on a piece of paper or computer screen.

Our brains also love learning about the places and spaces around us. Imagine being in a plain or helicopter and looking at the Earth from above. Have you ever played with a drone mounted with a video camera or looked at satellite images of where you live? If so, you will know how exciting it can be to see your house and the neighbourhood from above.

Suppose you are watching a TV documentary about a gigantic waterfall. Your brain will better understand and remember the details if you can see exactly where on a map this special place is.

Neuroscientists confirm that children who hear and use many spatial words like between, above, below and near earn higher test scores. These children also are better at reproducing spatial designs with blocks and at solving algebraic problems, such as 2 + ? = 7.

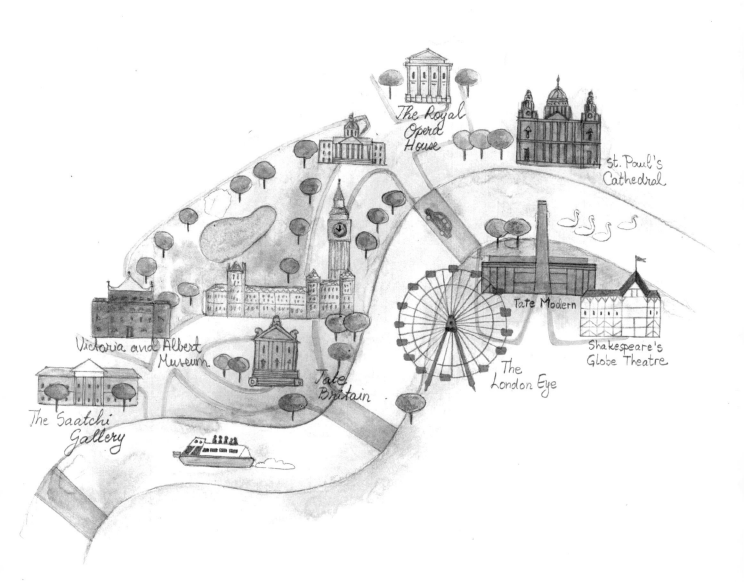

The Royal Opera House

St. Paul's Cathedral

Victoria and Albert Museum

Tate Modern

Tate Britain

The London Eye

Shakespeare's Globe Theatre

The Saatchi Gallery

TRY THIS:

Ask an adult about how to safely create experiments that will help you learn complicated ideas and concepts. You can play together and learn through cooking and baking. You can learn while observing plants, animals, birds or fish in different locations, both inside and outside. Try using tools and instruments to measure the weather, watch the night sky or work in the garden.

With adult supervision to keep you safe, there is so much you can do. Experiment with voice recorders, mirrors, sand or carpentry equipment. Create imaginary worlds using small toys. Find space to run and jump. Climb on ropes, ladders, nets and trees. Act out great events from history. Explore maths and science problems. Count, sort and classify anything that comes to hand: buttons, coins, pebbles, pieces of fabric, marbles. Try using different measuring methods and equipment: scales, cups, calendars, clocks, tape measures. Operate a cash register, use a computer, lace beads, play with magnets and puzzles.

Ask an adult to help you play with timelines, mind maps and maps of the land and sea.

Think about the important events in your life over the years. Can you make a timeline of them using words and images? What about creating a table-top timeline with your parents, using real objects like framed photographs and personal possessions, to create a physical timeline of your family history?
You can also learn to create the timeline of a process. Making pancakes, for example, or sandwiches, or brushing your teeth. Watch what members of your family do. Break it down into steps. Make a drawing for each step in the right order. It's helpful to divide a sheet of paper into four boxes for this task, using one box for each step.

Try creating a mind map for your birthday party. This will help you understand the whole party procedure. You can also try making a 'Sunday activities mind map', a 'Benefits of fruit mind map', then one for every school lesson.

Ask an adult to help you locate your house using Google Maps or a similar site that has a satellite view. Create a map of your room or classroom. Then try making one of the school playground. Once you are confident with your mapmaking, try creating one of the area where you live. When you can do that, you'll be ready to explore bigger maps of your own country, then of the entire world.

Watch the video tutorials at
http://www.howpeoplelearnbook.com/tutorials to learn how to create timelines and mind maps, as well as how to play with space maps.

Science story   10

HOW TO STOP THE PROCESS OF FORGETTING?

Remember the idea of the brain being like a big city? When you learn new things, it's like moving information into cars on roads, heading for specific houses. Similarly, when you want to fetch information that you learned a while ago, it's like a car going to that particular house, collecting the information and driving it on fast roads to get it to where you need it.

Now the question is, how do you keep the new information you learn in those houses for longer periods of time? When your teacher asks you about something you learned last week, how can you remember it?

Each of the houses has doors. When you store information in the house, you close the door behind you to keep it safe. When you need to access the information, you can open the door and retrieve it.

Scientists can teach us all kinds of techniques to help us store information. But they recommend that you visit the information you have stored often, otherwise you will forget it. If the car doesn't travel to a house often enough and the door stays closed for too long, the unused roads will disappear. The same happens with neural pathways in our brains: unused ones will disappear, and you will not remember the information when you need it.

TRY THIS:

Each time you learn something important, write a question about it on a piece of paper. Ask an adult to help you with the question if you need to. Put the question in a jar or another container. At the end of the week, take the pieces of paper out the jar and try to answer all of the questions. Do not worry if you do not remember the answers yet. Look up the answers you do not know in textbooks or online. This is an example of how information is housed in your brain to make sure that you do not forget.

You can have a jar for each week of the month. At the end of the month, move all of the questions into a box of the month. By the end of the year, you will have 12 boxes with questions concerning everything you've learned. Invite your classmates to use this strategy too. At the end of each month, mix the questions from your boxes and try answering them one by one. It doesn't matter how many answers you know. For your brain to stop the forgetting, it is important to revisit information on a weekly and monthly basis.

I know what you learn in your school is structured around subjects like maths, science, languages, history, geography, music, art and sport. You do not have to create different jars for each subject. In fact, your brain learns best when you ask it to jump from one subject to another, mixing up the questions.

Please, do not stop during your holidays. Your brain learns every day of the year, everywhere, not only in school. During the holidays, you might visit other members of your family, such as grandparents. They usually tell great stories. Get them involved in helping you create questions based on their stories. You might visit the seaside. Create questions about everything you observe and put it into your weekly jar. You might visit a museum. Again, another great opportunity to write questions about what you learn there.

During the holiday, try keeping a learning journal. Draw a small house each time you learn something new and write down next to it the important facts or stories. Later, in the evening, transform those facts and stories into questions for the jar.

Watch the video tutorial at http://www.howpeoplelearnbook.com/tutorials about how to choose the materials necessary for these learning techniques

DOODLE HERE:

TESTING DOESN'T NEED TO BE INITIATED BY THE TEACHER!

You probably have heard all about school tests by now. You may even have taken a few. You certainly know that parents and teachers can get anxious about them.

A test is a set of questions or problems that can help measure a person's knowledge or skills. Tests often are used by school teachers. But testing doesn't need to be initiated by them. You can have fun creating a test yourself and stimulate your brain while you do so.

First, remember we said there is no one area in the brain that is solely responsible for memory. Most of our memories are well distributed throughout the brain. This explains why you may have great recall for one subject, like English, and poor recall for another, like maths. Or you might be great with numbers and struggle with people's names. To help your brain stretch and grow, you can create your own tests and discover how much you have learned.

Creating materials like quizzes, flashcards and games that help you test your learning progress can be huge fun. Teachers, friends and family can all help you with this.

You have to be aware that self-quizzing can feel awkward and frustrating to start with. Re-reading information in a textbook will seem easier. This happens particularly when the new information you have learned is hard to recall.

What you will not sense, when struggling to retrieve a memory, is the fact that every time you work hard like this, you are strengthening the neural pathways in your brain. When you re-study something after failing to recall it, you actually learn it more effectively than if you had not tried to recall it.

When using flashcards, don't stop quizzing yourself on the cards that you answer correctly a couple of times. Continue to shuffle them into the deck. Revisit your cards periodically. Mixing maths cards with science cards and vocabulary cards will greatly improve your learning and is quite amusing.

TRY THIS:

You can use pictures from magazines or draw simple pictures to create flashcards.

Watch the video tutorial at http://www.howpeoplelearnbook.com/tutorials about what flashcards are and how to create your own. This includes flash-cards on multiplication, the alphabet, vocabulary and synonyms, as well as instructions about how to play and learn with them. The tutorial also will help you create your own quizzes and games. Watch it and testing will always be fun for you.

DOODLE HERE:

HOW THE ENVIRONMENT INFLUENCES LEARNING?

Let's try a short experiment. If you are in your room or a safe place, sit and close your eyes. Try to remember the objects around you and name them. How many do you remember? Quite a few, right? Especially if you are in a room you know well.

Your eyes are an important part of the learning process. Your eyes work from the moment you wake up to the moment you close them to go to sleep. They take in lots of information about the world around you: shapes, colours, movements and more. Then they send the information to your brain for processing, so the brain knows what's going on outside your body.

When you enter the classroom or your study room, your brain absorbs how the whole space comes together: floor, furniture, walls, everything. Scientists say that most learning occurs through the eyes. What do you see around you when you learn?

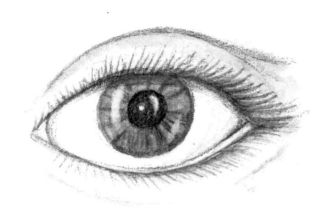

Although we are rarely consciously aware of it, sunlight, artificial lighting, room colour or a distant view of vegetation all can have a very powerful impact on learning. Your environment influences how and what you learn because humans experience the world through five senses: sight, but also hearing, touch, taste and smell. Our senses work together to give us a total picture of our experiences. Learning takes place when the brain is able to put together information from all the senses.

To help your brain learn most in a situation, you should involve as many of your senses as possible. Use toys and different materials to make information not only visible, but also touchable and smelly. If you are struggling with maths, ask for help from an adult and try using some blocks, LEGO bricks or other materials to create scenarios that will help you work out the maths problems. When a reading assignment seems boring, use tape, glue and craft materials to create a vivid 3D storyboard for what you are reading. Once you start, you can also choose background music that fits best with the storyline.

TRY THIS:

Create a unique learning area with a desk and bean bag. You never want to miss a learning opportunity just because you didn't have the right tools to hand. Stock your desk with different types of pens and pencils, rulers, erasers, paper and cards. Plus glue and scissors, if you are allowed.

You can put flashcards and posters on the walls. You can create these together with your friends and family. You might start with simple colours and numbers but, when you are older, you can add more complicated stuff like Shakespeare quotes and scientific equations.

Your brain will be inspired to create and learn in a space that has plenty of materials like wood blocks, hollow blocks, puzzles, LEGO bricks, musical instruments, a white board, white board markers and erasers, coloured masking tape, washable glue sticks, plastic adhesive, felt sheets, foam sheets, eye stickers, glitter, craft materials, pipe cleaners and buttons.

HOW TO FIGHT THE URGE TO DO IT LATER!

Over the past few years, I've asked several children like you how they feel when a parent or other adult tells them to clean their room or do their homework or asks them if they have completed a task. More often than not, the children tell me, these commands and enquiries make them think 'Why this again?', 'I hate homework!' and, in particular, 'I'll do it later!'

Let's have a look inside the brain of a child and see what happens when the adults in your life encourage you to do school work or household chores and all you want to do is put it off until later.

Remember we talked about this small part of the brain, the amygdala? It is part of the emotional brain and regulates cravings and desires. The amygdala is concerned with immediate pleasure not really caring about the future.

On the other hand, there is the prefrontal cortex, the decision-making centre located behind your forehead. It is exhaustible, tiring quickly. The prefrontal cortex requires training to work more effectively.

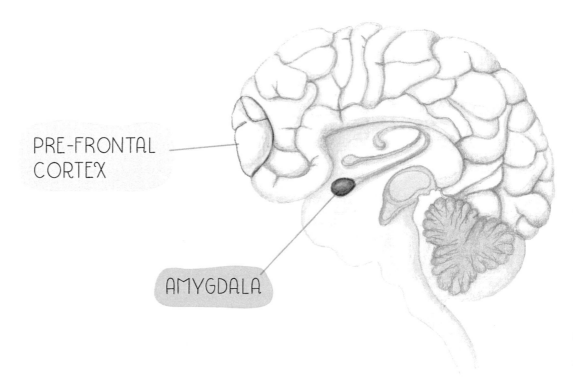

PRE-FRONTAL CORTEX

AMYGDALA

The 'I'll do it later' thought occurs when the pleasure-seeking, emotional brain acts too quickly for the rational prefrontal cortex to catch up. The emotional brain pushes you towards abandoning the stressful task in favour of a more rewarding one.

Scientists call the impulse to put things off until later procrastination. When an activity seems particularly challenging or overwhelming for your brain, the amygdala is activated to protect you from negative feelings. This is how, all of a sudden, spending some time watching TV becomes a more appealing idea for your brain than working on a homework assignment.

Try observing how the two parts of your brain fight over your thoughts. Once you are able to observe this fight, it is up to you to decide which part of the brain wins. 'There's something better to do,' the emotional brain will say. If you let it win, you'll put off your chores and homework assignments, opting instead to hang out with friends, watch TV or play on your smartphone.

You'll have fun but doing those activities more than others will not help your brain develop well. Since the emotional brain likes to repeat those actions that bring pleasure, you will be encouraged by one part of your brain to continue with these habits even if only focusing on them is not good for you in the long term.

Procrastination also results from your brain's need to protect itself from the fear of failure. In order not to fail at a task, your brain prefers to not perform it at all. Very often your brain will decide to put off chores, homework or other duties simply because it doesn't understand what is expected of you. When your brain is unsure about your exact role or it feels you do not have the skill set to tackle a job, it is not likely to want to take it on.

If a parent or other adult has assigned you a chore, ask them to take the time to show you exactly how to complete it, step by step. You can observe them do it, learn from them and even make suggestions on how to improve the task and make it easier.

Adults can also help you deal with troubling homework assignments, providing a little tutoring. A chart or a daily schedule of your tasks can help keep you on track and avoid procrastination.

If you observe that your emotional brain is putting things off because of fear of failure, ask a parent or a teacher to help you fight that feeling. Remember what brain scientists say about how the brain learns and grows? They say that practice is the best teacher.

Your brain definitely needs a little time after school to relax before it takes on additional studies. Adults know that. Create a schedule together with your parents and then ask for their help to stick to it.

TRY THIS:

When an adult tells you to do a chore, ask them to be more specific about what needs to be done. For example, if you have been told to clean the playroom, discover what exactly is expected. Does it mean picking up balls off the floor? Rearranging books on shelves? What else?

Confront the myth of moods. Sometimes your emotional brain will try to evade a task by saying, 'I'm not in the mood to do that now. I'll wait until the urge strikes.' Don't let it get away with it. Self-discipline is important. The prefrontal cortex can help you with that.

Create a calendar or to-do list for daily activities. The great news is your emotional brain loves the feeling of crossing off completed items because this provides a sense of achievement and confidence.

Tackle distasteful tasks first, so your brain feels a sense of relief. Starting is the biggest hurdle for your brain.

Break tasks down into manageable parts. Cleaning a room includes steps such as picking up toys or clothing, then dusting, followed by vacuuming.

Your brain will love positive posters with mottoes to live by, such as 'You can do it!' or 'Where there's a will there's a way!'

Create the right atmosphere. When physical labour is required, lively music can rev up everyone's brain. However, music or TV during homework is a distraction for your brain and should be avoided.

WHAT TO DO IF YOUR BRAIN DOESN'T LIKE SCHOOL?

When I ask children like you why they sometimes dislike school, very often I hear the same responses: 'I do not understand why we have to learn about a lot of the things we study.' 'Many of the subjects are unclear to me.' 'Our teacher is very demanding and tough.' 'Kids who think they are smarter bother me.' 'Sometimes school feels like prison, because we are not allowed to move or talk for ages.' 'Not all kids are friendly.' 'I feel I don't belong there.'

If you ever feel like this, talk to an adult about it. Brain scientists say it may happen when some of the important needs of our brains are not being met. Let me help you understand when it happens, so that you and your family know how to manage those feelings.

Scientists tell us that when the fun stops, learning often stops too. Unfortunately, in some schools, teachers are pressured to work in classrooms with children on the same page, in the same book, sitting in straight rows, facing straight ahead. Many wrongly assume that children who are laughing, interacting in groups or being creative with art, music or dance are not involved in proper learning. The truth is that when joy and comfort is erased from the classroom, your brain learns a lot less.

Brain studies also teach us that the presence of bullies and authoritarian teachers in the classroom makes learning very difficult. The amygdala in your emotional brain is very sensitive to threats. When stress takes over the emotional part of the brain, the rational brain is not able to process information and learn effectively.

Scientists also suggest that the brain is not interested in learning if the information is not relevant. To be interested, your brain has to be able to answer the question 'Why are we learning about this?' at any point in a lesson. The brain also gets totally disengaged by unclear lessons and irrelevant exercises that fail to provide certainty around learning goals.

If you ever feel that school is like prison, it may be because you don't have much autonomy while you are there. This happens when you must spend more time doing exactly what you are told to do rather than deciding exactly how and what you want to learn. Simply put, autonomy means feeling, behaving and thinking independently of others. Human brains are naturally designed to explore and play freely. Structure is good, but too much structure and a lack of choice rob your brain of the joy of discovery.

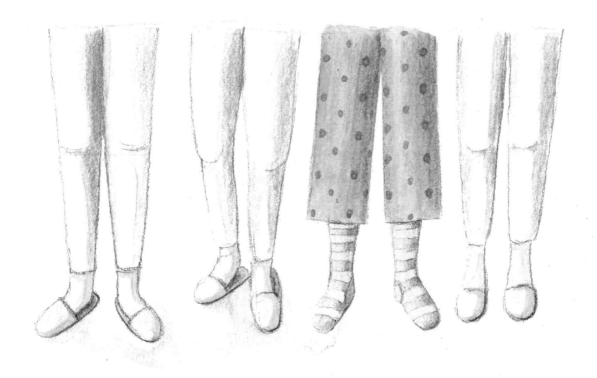

It is also very difficult for a brain to learn and enjoy school when it feels a teacher or a friend favours other people more than you. This usually happens when a brain doesn't feel a sense of connection and relatedness with others. It can result in a lack of confidence and self-doubt. Talk to an adult about it if you feel this way.

When unfair things happen, you might get frustrated with teachers about homework assignments or grades. You might feel that rules are only applied for some kids, or that rewards and praise are given only to certain classmates. It is very important to speak up. Talk to your parents first, when you feel this way. The emotional part of the human brain is very sensitive to unfairness. That's where all these feelings are coming from.

TRY THIS:

If you don't like school, the first step is to find out why. Play the detective and create two lists: one about the situations, assignments or people that upset you, one about the things you enjoy. Ask an adult to help you manage what is on your negative list and to remind you to be grateful for what is on the positive one.

Find answers to following questions:
Would remembering to do your homework help you feel more confident if you're called on in class?
How can you get help with school work that's difficult?
Could you find a way to show off your special interests and talents?
If you made just one new friend, would you feel less alone?
If you helped someone else feel less alone, would you feel even better yourself? Which activities could you try that would help you make new friends?

HOW TO HELP YOUR BRAIN GROW, STAY FIT AND STRONG?

What if, during school hours, you and your classmates were not sitting at desks but walking on treadmills? Can you imagine yourself listening to the explanation of a maths problem or studying English on treadmills fashioned to accommodate textbooks or computers? Brain scientists tell us that treadmills in the classroom might harness the valuable advantage of increasing the oxygen supply naturally, as well as all the other advantages of regular exercise.

Take a big deep breath...ahhh...Oxygen. This colourless, odourless and tasteless element is vital to all living things. Oxygen is in the air we breathe.

There are scientific experiments showing that when children like you exercise aerobically during school, their brains work better. These experiments suggest that the level of fitness is not as important as a steady increase in oxygen supply to the brain.

Now, let's talk about sleep. Every night, parents around the world can be heard saying, 'Go to bed, NOW!' How does this make you feel when you hear it? As every child knows, fights over bedtime can be one of the biggest power struggles you'll have with your parents.

The truth is, adults simply do not understand how difficult it is to go to bed at night. They don't appreciate how many things you are going to miss by going to sleep. Or they are unaware that you are frightened of the dark. Sometimes, you simply want to be in control and decide for yourself when it's best to go to bed.

I agree. You should learn to prepare yourself for sleep and decide independently when it's the best time. To help you to make a good decision, let me provide you with some data from brain scientists. Researchers tell us that sleep loss equals brain drain. They say that if we take an A student your age and insist that she has just under seven hours of sleep each night, in less than a month she will not be an A student anymore.

Brain scientists know that a lack of sleep will prevent your brain from working properly. It's almost as if, without sleep, the lights in your brain's city shut down and you can't commit new experiences to memory. Loss of sleep impacts attention, thinking, decision-making, memory, mood and even movement. When you are asleep, the neurones in your brain show vigorous activity. It's like brain cells are trying to replay what you learned that day.

When memory of an event is first represented in the brain, it is fragile and vulnerable to being lost. Studies suggest that sleep helps make our memories more permanent. If I were a teacher, I would assign sleep as part of your homework every day. During sleep, new information learned in school and elsewhere is organised by the brain. New lessons and experiences are stored as long-term memories.

Brain studies also suggest that sleep is often disrupted by our use of technology. Experiments show that children using computers, tablets, TVs, smartphones and other devices for more than two hours a day can experience sleep loss and consequently memory loss.

Having trouble sleeping is also a sign of stress. If you're not getting enough sleep, you probably feel grouchy and tired during the day. Feeling tired can make your school day seem even worse. If you're stressed, you might have a hard time making decisions. In the morning, you can't decide what to eat, what to wear or what to pack for lunch. You don't want to go to school, so you put off getting your stuff together.

Many children I talk to also say their mood gets worse and worse when they go too long without eating. Did that ever happen to you?

Brain scientists tell us that nutrition is just as important for the brain as for the body. A well-fed brain is more likely to result in a positive mood, good behaviour and receptiveness to learning. The brains of young children like you need a regular supply of energy so that they can think effectively. There is evidence that eating breakfast is more beneficial to learning than not having breakfast.

Our brains and bodies need nearly 40 different nutrients. The more varied our diet is, the more likely it is that we get enough of everything we need. It is really important that we drink lots of water too. Research demonstrates that a lack of water can lead to fatigue, dizziness, anger, poor concentration and reduced thinking abilities, all of which affect learning.

Let's place our fists together again in order to measure the average size of our brain. The brain is composed of mostly fat and water. The water you drink daily detoxifies the body and the brain by enhancing circulation and removing waste that would impede memory and concentration. Nourishing your brain with water will help it stay fit and strong. This is key to your learning performance.

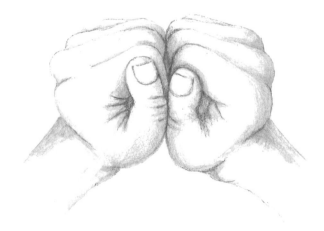

TRY THIS:

Our brains were built for walking. To improve your thinking skills, move! Start your day with a long walk. When you are in school, make sure you go outside between classes.

Every time your teacher invites you to participate in thinking games that require movement, say yes. Feel free to jump, skip and sing rhymes if it's required. Those exercises are meant to help your brain learn better. If your teacher doesn't ever do that, you could ask for permission to move around, stretch or change posture.

Have quiet time before bedtime. Ideally, bedtime should be a time of quiet throughout the house – no loud TV or music, no sibling arguments. Make sure that you do not play video games or go on the computer, tablet or smartphone for at least 30 minutes before bedtime.

Set your own alarm clock at night when you think it is the best time for your brain to go to bed. Set another alarm to wake you up in the morning. Make sure you use a subtle alarm tone that doesn't rattle your nerves.

Ask your parents if you can have a soft light in the room for 30 minutes before lights out. For children your age, reading or taking a warm bath is a good way to help you fall asleep. Try to go to bed at the same time every night. This helps your body get into a routine.

Limit foods and drinks that contain caffeine. These include some fizzy drinks and things like iced tea. Don't have a TV in your room. Research shows that kids who have one in their room sleep less.

Don't exercise just before going to bed. Do exercise earlier in the day. This helps you sleep better. Use your bed only for sleeping, not for homework, playing games or talking on the phone. That way, you'll train your body to associate your bed with sleep.

Watch the video tutorial at http://www.howpeoplelearnbook.com/tutorials about how to make a Sleep Chart poster. Make your own and use it to record the number of hours you sleep each night.

Run an experiment to see for yourself the importance of water. Ask your parents to help you purchase two plants that look exactly the same. Place the two plants in a sunny spot and water one of them but not the other. Over the next few days, observe what happens to the plant that doesn't get any water. What do you see? Once you've observed the results, start watering the second plant too and help it recover.

Make sure you take on lots of water yourself. A bottle or cup with a fun design, that you carry with you all the time, can encourage you to drink more water and take care of your brain.

Did you know that dark-coloured urine is a sign of dehydration? If you drink a healthy amount of water, your pee will be a very pale yellow. This fun fact might just be gross enough to motivate you to drink lots every day.

Set a family goal to drink more water, so you can work on it together. Track your progress using an app, a sticker chart or even by marking your water bottles.

Watch the video tutorial at http://www.howpeoplelearnbook.com/tutorials about how to make a Water Chart poster. Make your own and use it to record how much water your drink each day.

DOODLE HERE:

24-DAY CHALLENGE!

Imagine that I ask you to do some squats. How many squats can you do in a minute? Do you remember what your body feels like after intense physical activity?

What if I ask you to look at some sweets for as long as you can before eating them? How long can you do that? Do you think you'll have the same sensation in your body the following day as you did after the squats?

How would you answer to these questions? Are you less honest if it will keep you out of trouble? Are you doing the right things even when others tease you about them? Do you complete your homework even when you find it difficult? When someone apologises, do you give them a second chance?

You can exercise your brain in different ways. Physical activities like swimming, running, walking and dancing are very good for muscles, bones and brains. Exercising patience, making good decisions, being able to intentionally focus your mind on something and resist distractions will help your mental strength.

The brain responds to activity just as muscles do. The brain grows with use and atrophies with inactivity. As you apply and exercise your mind, the neurons in your brain connect to one another in dense networks.

So, how about a 24-day brain challenge?

Each morning read one of the statements below. Focus on stretching your brain in that area during the day. Then, before you go to bed in the evening, answer the corresponding question.

Give it a go now!

DAY 1

Your brain learns when you try new things and take calculated risks even when you feel afraid. Talk to an adult about it and try it out.

 What new things did you learn today that required a calculated risk? How did you feel about overcoming fear?

_____

_____

DAY 2

Your brain learns when you work hard to complete what you start without getting upset even when everything falls apart.

 Was the work you did today hard to complete? Have you succeeded in managing the agitation that causes?

_____

_____

DAY 3

Your brain learns when you take responsibility for your actions and you are not looking to blame somebody else.

 What did you take responsibility for today?

_____

_____

DAY 4

Your brain learns when you seek out the positive rather than looking for everything that is wrong.

 What did you enjoy today? What are you grateful for?

_____

_____

DAY 5

Your brain learns when you show others that you care.

 In what ways did you pay attention to other people today? Did you help a classmate, friend or neighbour?

_____

_____

DAY 6

Your brain learns when you go out of your way to help someone in need or merely try to cheer someone up.

 Whom did you help today? How?

_____

_____

DAY 7

Your brain learns when you pay attention to what others think and feel, when you try to understand someone else's way of looking at a situation, even if you see it differently.

 Was there a moment today when you realised that your teacher, classmate or friend might think differently than you? Do you understand why they think that way?

DAY 8

Your brain learns when you look at the world around you with wonder and awe, when you are amazed by nature, arts, music, poems, and even the design of everyday things.

 What made you experience wonder today? Do you experience the same feeling when you look at the sky and start to think about how big the universe is?

DAY 9

Your brain learns when you are being thankful for what you have and who you are.

 How many times did you say 'Thank you' today?

_____

_____

DAY 10

Your brain learns when you imagine for yourself a future that is bright like a star.

 What's the most beautiful thing you see when you think about your future?

_____

_____

DAY 11

Your brain learns when you try to see the funny side of life where others may see none, when you laugh and have fun, but not at the expense of other people.

 What's the funniest joke or story you told or heard today?

_____

_____

DAY 12

Your brain learns when you talk to your friends or relatives about what's really important in life, about what you enjoy and what changes you want to make in the world.

 What meaningful conversation did you have today? What did you discover during it?

_____

_____

DAY 13

Your brain learns a lot when you practice self-control each and every day, when you patiently wait your turn, or calm down to avoid blurting out what you have to say.

 When did you exercise self-control today? How did it go?

_____

_____

DAY 14

Your brain learns when you are thoughtful about what you say and avoid hurting other people's feelings.

 Was there a moment today when you were mindful of other people?

_____

_____

DAY 15

Your brain learns when you do your best, remaining true to yourself and not putting on a show or bragging and boasting to make yourself feel good.

 Was there a moment today when you were intentionally modest?

_____

_____

DAY 16

Your brain learns when you give others a second chance and do not hold a grudge.

 Did anyone upset you today? Did you try to understand what prompted their behaviour? Did you manage to avoid holding it against them?

_____

_____

DAY 17

Your brain learns when you take charge, without taking over, by encouraging and guiding those who need you to be the leader.

 Were you a leader today? How exactly did you lead others and why?

_____

_____

DAY 18

Your brain learns when you decide to do what's right for everyone and not just for yourself.

 Was there a moment today when you decided to do what was the best for the team?

_____

_____

DAY 19

Your brain learns greatly every time you work in a team and do your share.

 How did you contribute today?

_____

_____

DAY 20

Your brain learns when you take time to think things through and decide for yourself.

 What did you decide to do today that is important for your health and well-being?

_____

_____

DAY 21

Your brain learns something new every second, wherever you go, whatever you do.

 What activities consumed your brain energy today?

_____

_____

DAY 22

Your brain learns when you listen to what others have to say and change your mind when new facts come your way.

 Did anyone convince you of anything new today? How and why did you change your mind?

_____

_____

DAY 23

Your brain learns when you ask questions, experiment, play or observe closely.

 What did you discover that surprised you today?

_____

_____

DAY 24

Your brain learns when you let your imagination soar, dream about new ways of living, invent and create.

 Did you come up with a new idea, invention or creation today? What's it about? Did you talk to anyone about it?

_____

_____

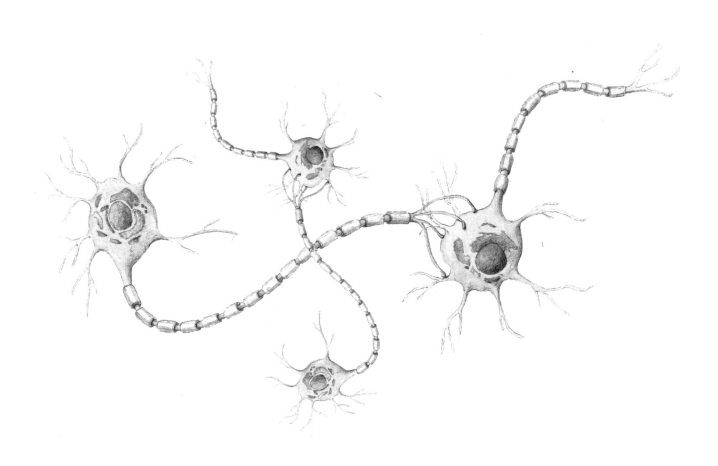

Bonus 2

17-DAY  CHALLENGE!

Imagine having only one container of water for your garden or house plants. No matter how much water you use, the container keeps refilling. Unfortunately, the world doesn't work like that. In fact, in some countries, good-quality, fresh water can run out very quickly.

Similarly, there are limits to other natural resources that humans use and have depended on for a long time. In some cases, it may take hundreds or thousands of years for them to run out completely, but it is certain that they will disappear in the end. In other cases, some of these resources are already in short supply. They are proving harder to find, with not enough available for those who need them.

In addition to taking care of natural resources, countries all over the world have tried to do something about waste. How much stuff does your family throw away? How much is recycled? Have you ever thought about taking care of something bought for you so well that it lasts as long as possible? Do you try to ensure that it can be repaired, updated, or broken down into smaller reusable elements when it reaches the end of its lifespan?

If you really care about the future of our planet and of humanity, why not have a go at the following 17-day challenge? As you now know, your brain learns best not only when you are reading and studying, but when you pay attention, care, do, experiment.

Enjoy the challenge and share with friends and family the marvellous things you learn along the way!

DAY 1

Your brain learns when you pay attention to what is healthy
– food, air, water – and when you are willing to teach others
about it. Check the ingredients on the labels of three types
of food in your fridge. Then, with an adult, search online for
information about these ingredients to learn how healthy they

DAY 2

Your brain learns when you question whether all children
around the world have access to sufficient nutritious food
in order to grow up healthy. Do some research and find out
about a place where food is scarce. Ask an adult about how
you might help someone in need of good nutrition.

DAY 3

Your brain learns when you can attend school but also when you ask why some children cannot because of poverty, disability or conflict. Find out if there is someone in your community unable to attend school for heath or other reasons and offer to learn together.

DAY 4

Your brain learns when you are allowed to pursue any profession, no matter your gender. Think of a profession where you see more women or more men employed. Why do you think that happens? What do you think might happen if the opposite sex were employed instead? What would the positive consequences be?

DAY 5

Your brain learns when you realise that life without water is impossible and you help adults preserve it and use it carefully. Observe and find three ways for your family to use less water over the next three weeks.

DAY 6

Your brain learns when you pay attention to the things you use at home or in school that require electricity. Do some research, then create a list of the top three sources of renewable and clean energy.

DAY 7

Your brain learns when you want to contribute your talents and skills towards solving some of the major problems our planet faces. If kids had jobs, what would yours be? What are you good at? How can you do more of that today?

DAY 8

Your brain learns when you pay close attention to the products and toys you use. Do some research and discover whether any of the ones you use are harmful to other people or the planet when thrown away.

DAY 9

Your brain learns when you notice things that seem unfair for certain people and you think about what can be done to make things fairer. What do you think it is like to have lots of money or to have very little? What difference does it make? Discuss with your family.

DAY 10

Your brain learns when you think about things that can make cities safer, healthier and friendlier for children, adults and animals. Think of one thing that could make the streets to your school safer for you and other children.

DAY 11

Your brain learns when you think about the small things you could do in your daily life that would help consume fewer resources. What do you think is the eco-friendlier product: a book or a tablet computer? Research online and discuss with your family.

DAY 12

Your brain learns when you wonder what 'climate change' means and why it is bad for our planet. Research or ask an adult to explain.

DAY 13

Your brain learns when you discover the importance of the ocean and why it is important that it is protected. Research and find two things that you use that come from the ocean.

DAY 14

Your brain learns when you ask what children can do to help protect other species and their habitats. Research and make a list of the endangered species in your own country.

DAY 15

Your brain learns when you feel safe at home and in school and when you ask adults what can be done so that you live in a safer world with less violence. Think about an occasion when you have not felt safe. Talk to an adult about it.

DAY 16

Your brain learns when you collaborate and work in teams on local or international projects. Partner with some friends for the next challenge and work together to accomplish the task.

DAY 17

Your brain learns when you ask yourself why there are homeless people and beggars. Ask an adult why some people are unable to earn enough money to pay for food or a place to live.

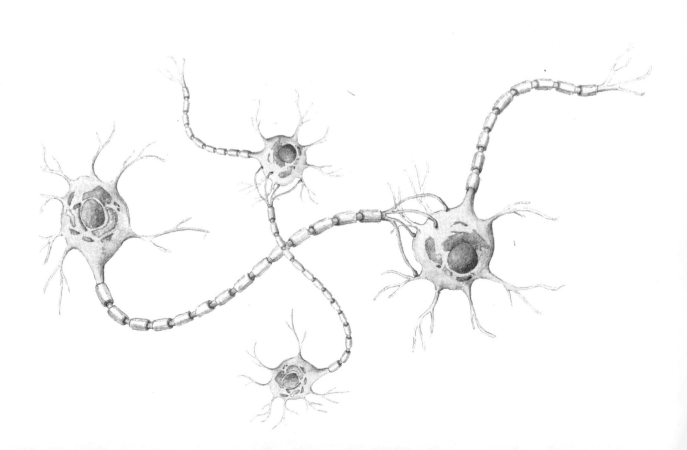

Coming soon

HOW PEOPLE LEARN GAME

What is one thing you wish you could change about the world?

Share favouri

Brain scientists say that boredom can be caused by _____ and disinterest in the details of a task.

Your environm and what you humans exper through five sight, but al and smell. T most in a s involve as

If on w

What kind of toy or object do you wish you could make?

HOW PEOPLE LEARN GAME

© 2019 Copyright Olimpia Mesa

Name two things you can do when you begin to feel bored.

fight the thing later.

ts tell us that ins learn most sily in a e environment an _____ things for

the brain grow hening neural ontinue and going to lty. rain's

158

www.howpeoplelearnbook.com

=> VISIT WEBSITE

Made in the USA
San Bernardino, CA
20 August 2019